LYNN FREEMAN OLSO

Audience Pleasers

A special collection of 11 favorite solos for piano students at the late elementary to early intermediate levels

BOOK 2

Late Elementary to Early Intermediate

The magic continues in this second volume of Lynn Freeman Olson's AUDIENCE PLEASERS. Discover for yourself the delightful melodies and exciting rhythms that make his music unforgettable. Turn the page, and let the enchantment of another collection of Lynn Freeman Olson's solos begin!

Alfred

A Gentle Joke

Lynn Freeman Olson

Italian Festival

Lynn Freeman Olson

Commissioned by the
Hattiesburg Piano Teacher's League

Rondo Capriccio

Lynn Freeman Olson

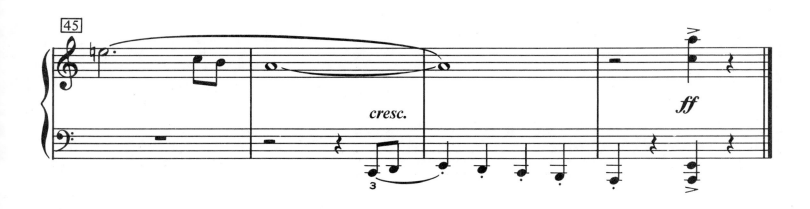

Mountain Railway

Lynn Freeman Olson

Garden Pools in Kyoto

Lynn Freeman Olson

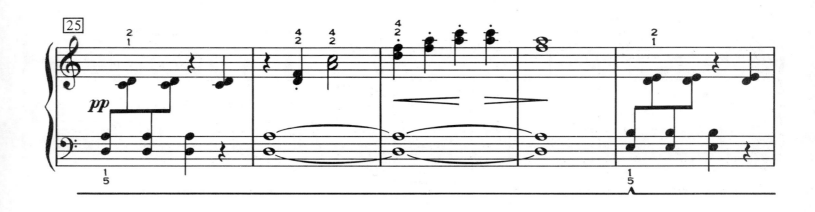

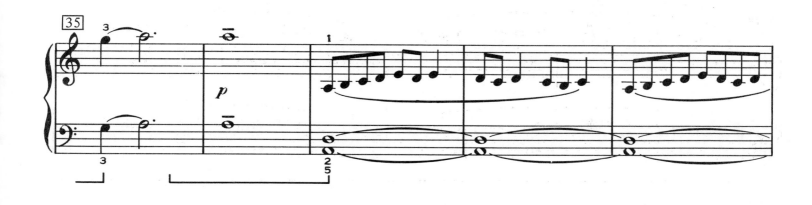

Popcorn

Lynn Freeman Olson

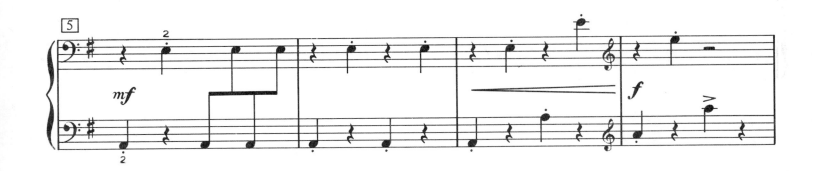

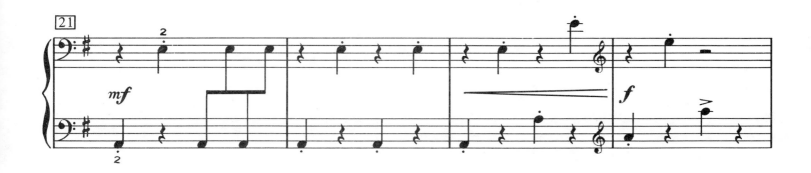

Old Tale

Lynn Freeman Olson

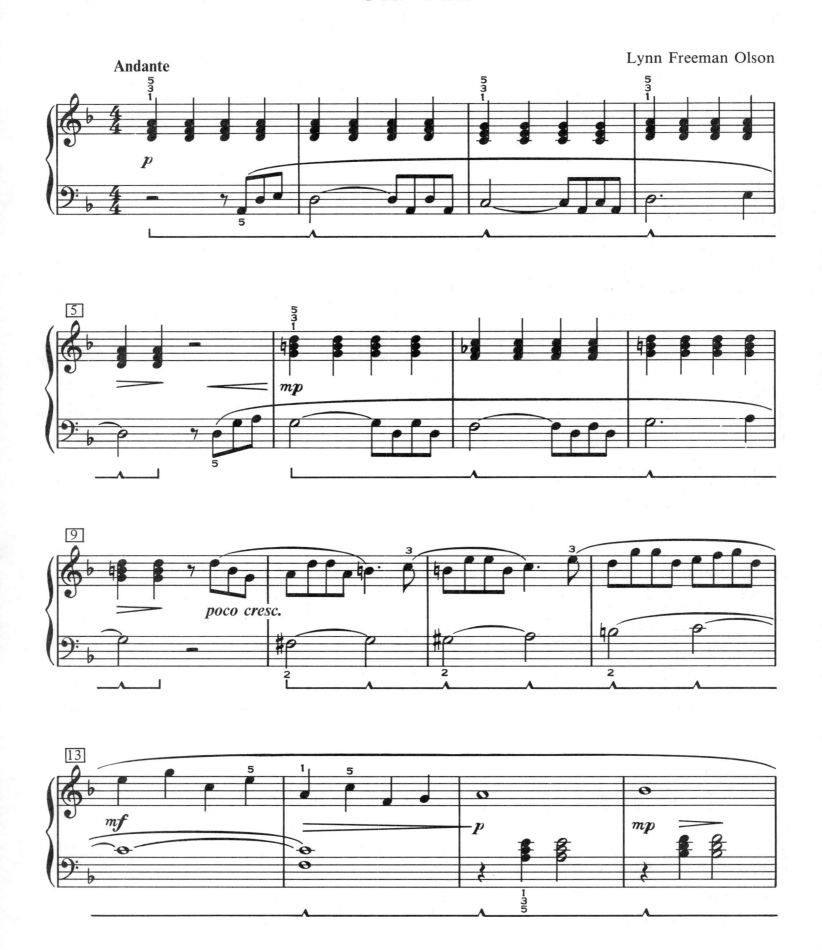

Starlight Mood

Lynn Freeman Olson

*Or play each 3rd with the same pair of fingers, if you like ($\frac{4}{2}$ or $\frac{3}{1}$).

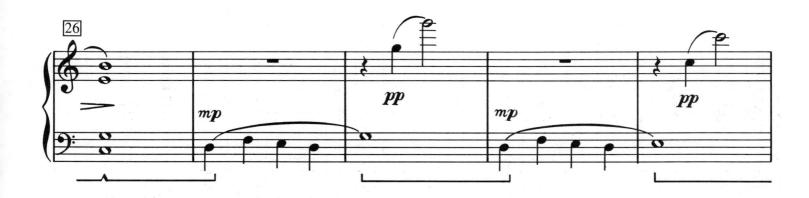

The Pines

Lynn Freeman Olson

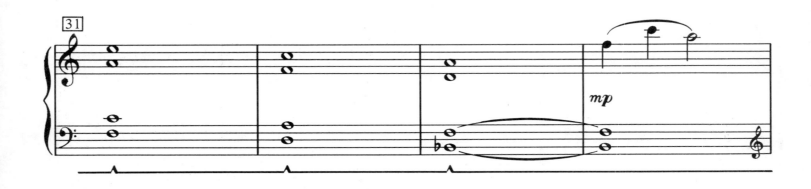

The Water Is Wide

British Isles Folksong
Arr. Lynn Freeman Olson

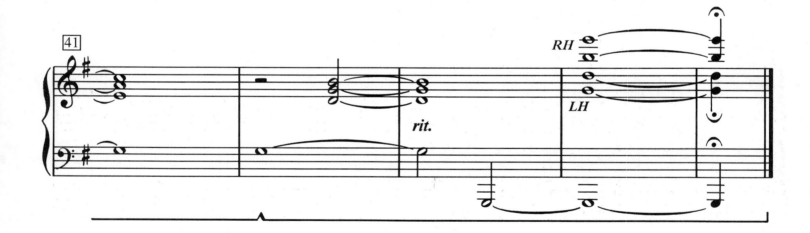

The water is wide, yet I must go.
Oh, would that I had wings to fly!
Is there a boat that will carry two?
Then both may go, my love and I.

A ship that sails out on the sea
Is loaded deep, deep as she can be,
Yet not so deep as the love I'm in—
I know not if I sink or swim.

Sword Dance

Lynn Freeman Olson

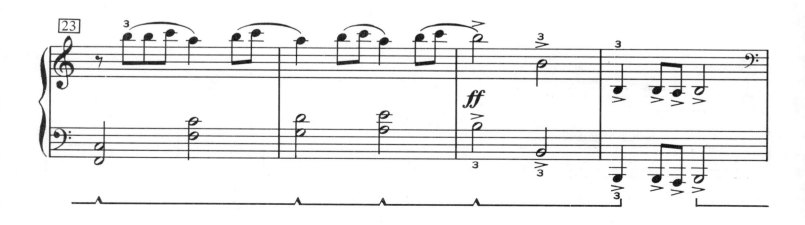